dedicated to the development of stability operations capabilities.[9] A significant investment has been made in CA force structure for this low density, high demand capability. Since September 11, 2001, the force will have more than doubled from an authorized strength of approximately 5631 to 11718.[10]

Unfortunately, the growth in Civil Affairs force structure has not been accompanied by a corresponding effort to increase the quality of the force. Civil Affairs gaps in capability and capacity are evident by difficulty filling requirements in multiple theaters, use of "in lieu of" fills from other services for current operations, the stand-up of ad hoc CA-like capabilities, and the unavailability of Civil Affairs functional experts.[11] This paper will address the challenges associated with fielding fully trained Army Reserve CA functional specialists. The Army CA force lacks the functional specialist capacity and capability required to support stability operations activities of the Joint Force Commander as well as broader USG programs aimed at building the capacity of a partner nation's government in the areas of rule of law, economic development, governance, public health and welfare, infrastructure, and public education and information.

Overview of Functional Specialties

Approximately 94% of the U.S. Department of Defense's Civil Affairs capability resides in the Army due to the fact that interaction with the civilian sector is primarily associated with land warfare.[12] The majority of these forces, approximately 90%, are currently in the U.S. Army Reserve. There are no CA units in the Army National Guard. Programmed growth in the Active Component (AC) to rebalance the CA force will change the ratio to 72% Reserve Component (RC) and 28% AC by 2014. Traditionally, the majority of CA units have been in the Army Reserve to capitalize on the unique capabilities of citizen soldiers who can offer high levels of civilian expertise in functions such as agriculture, public administration, and economics as well as the military education appropriate to their grade.[13] The significant difference between Army AC and United States Army Reserve (USAR) CA organizational structure is the CA functional specialty capabilities residing in USAR CA units.

The CA branch competencies consist of generalists and functional specialists. Generalists are well versed in common CA skill sets CA such as preventing civilian interference with military operations, providing CA staff augmentation, analyzing the civil component of the area of operations, and planning and managing small scale quick impact projects and programs. Most active duty CA staff personnel and personnel assigned to tactical units in the USAR are CA generalists. When employed, CA generalists support the commander's immediate needs by preventing civilian interference with military operations, mobilizing civilian resources to support military operations, and conducting humanitarian operations. CA functional specialists provide additional areas of expertise, normally acquired through civilian education, training, and experience. Functional specialists leverage their civilian skills and expertise to assist USG efforts in rebuilding systems, infrastructure, and ministries or support requirements for civil-military teaming.[14] CA core tasks involve the application of CA functional specialty skills in areas normally the responsibility of civil government to enhance the conduct of Civil Military Operations.[15] By their very nature, these tasks require skills that must come from the reserve component because they cannot be cost effectively maintained in the active component.

Current CA doctrine lists 14 functional specialties organized into six functional specialty areas. The functional specialists are organized into teams that plan and enable host nation government operations across the following six areas: rule of law, economic stability, infrastructure, governance, public health and welfare, and public education and information as defined in table 1.

Rule of Law	Economic Stability	Infrastructure
Rule of law pertains to the fair, competent, and efficient application and fair and effective enforcement of the civil and criminal laws of a society through impartial legal institutions and competent police and corrections systems. This functional area includes judge advocates trained in international and comparative law as well as CA specialists in related subjects.	*Economic stability* pertains to the efficient management (for example, production, distribution, trade, and consumption) of resources, goods, and services to ensure the viability of a society's economic system. This discipline includes CA specialists in economic development, civilian supply, and food and agriculture.	*Infrastructure* pertains to designing, building, and maintaining the organizations, systems, and architecture required to support transportation, water, communications, and power. This discipline includes CA specialists in public transportation, public works and utilities, and public communication
Governance	Public Health and Welfare	Public Education and Information
Governance pertains to creating, resourcing, managing, and sustaining the institutions and processes through which a society is governed, is protected, and prospers. This discipline includes CA specialists in public administration, environmental management, and public safety areas.	*Public health and welfare* pertains to the systems, institutions, programs, and practices that promote the physical, mental, and social well-being of a society. This discipline includes CA specialists in public health and cultural relations	*Public education and information* pertains to designing, resourcing, and implementing public education and public information programs and systems through media and formal education institutions. This discipline includes CA specialists in public education and civil information

Table 1. Army Civil Affairs Functional Specialty Areas.

The Army designates skill identifiers (SI) for 11 of the functional specialties some of which are no longer in CA doctrine: Civil Defense Officer (5Y), Economist (6C), Public Education Officer (6D), Civilian Supply Officer (6E), Public Transportation Officer (6F), Public Facilities Officer (6G), Public Safety Officer (6H), Public Communication Officer (6R), Agricultural Officer (6U), Cultural Affairs Officer (6V), and Archivist (6W). The skill identifiers were intended to establish standards and qualifications for the specialties and allow identification and tracking of officers with specialties in the CA force. The standards for awarding of a skill identifier are generally based on some combination of education and/or experience broadly related to the specialty. For example, the qualifications for a public safety officer are "bachelor degree in criminology, fire science, police science, corrections management, or public administration and/or 3 years practical experience in a supervisory or management position in a government related public safety field or equivalent private industry position."[16] Only 309 or 40% of the 780 positions designated as functional specialties within the reserve force structure have skill identifiers associated with them. Army Medical and Judge Advocate General Branches fill 294 or 31% of the specialty positions. Twelve percent of the positions are filled by CA plans or operations NCOs for which there are no functional specialty skill identifiers. The remaining 11% of the positions are filled by CA officer generalists for which there are no skill identifiers associated.

USAR CA Command (CACOM) Functional Specialties Cell, 31 personnel per cell, 3 cells per CACOM O6 38A, Team Chief/Plans Officer E9 38B 2S, Operations NCO					
Rule of Law Section -O5 38A 6H, Public Safety Officer -O5 27A, International Law Officer -O5 38A 6E, Property Resource Control Officer -E7 38B402S, CA Plans NCO	Economic Stability Section -O5 38A 6U, Agriculture Officer -O5 38A 6C, Commerce Officer -O5 38A 6C, Economic Functions Officer -O5 38A 6C, Price Control/Rations Officer -E7 38B402S, CA Plans NCO	Infrastructure Section -O5 38A 6G, Public Works Officer (Utilities) -O5 38A 6G, Public Works Officer (Facilities) -O5 38A 6R, Public Communications Officer -O5 38A 6F, Public Transportation Officer -E7 38B402S, CA Plans NCO	Governance Section -O5 38A , Public Administration Officer -O5 38A 6E, Civil Supply Officer -O5 27A, International Law Officer -O5 38A 6V, Cultural Affairs Officer -E8 38B502S, CA Plans NCO	Public Health Section -O5 60C, Public Health Officer -O5 64B, Vet Preventative Medicine -O5 70H, Medical Plans & Operations -O5 70K, Health Facilities Planner -O5 72D, Environmental Sciences -O5 66B , Community Health Nurse -E8 38B50W42S, Public Health NCO	Public Education and Information Section -O5 38A 6D, Public Education Officer -O5 38A , Civil Information Officer -E7 38B402S, Plans NCO
USAR CA Brigade Functional Specialties Cell, 16 personnel per cell, 1 cell per brigade O6 38A, Team Chief/Plans Officer E8 38B2S, Operations NCO					
Rule of Law Section -O5 38A 6H, Public Safety Officer -O4 27A, International Law Officer -O4 38A 6E, Property Resource Control Officer		Infrastructure Section -O5 38A 6G, Public Works Officer (Utilities) -O4 38A 6G, Public Works Officer (Facilities) -O5 38A 6R, Public Communications Officer	Governance Section -O5 38A 6E, Civil Supply Officer -O4 38A, Public Administration Officer -E7 38B2S, Plans NCO	Public Health Section -O5 60C, Public Health Officer -O5 64B, Vet Preventative Medicine -O5 70H, Medical Plans & Operations -O4 72D, Environmental Sciences -E8 68W, Public Health NCO	
USAR CA Battalion Functional Specialties Cell, 8 personnel per cell, 1 cell per battalion O4 38A, Civil Affairs (Generalist)					
-O4 27A3N, International Law Officer -O4 38A 6H, Public Safety Officer		-O4 38A 6G, Public Works Officer (Utilities)	-O4 38A 6E, Civil Supply Officer	-O4 60C, Public Health Officer -O4 64B, Vet Preventative Medicine -E8 68W2S, Public Health NCO	

Table 2. Army Civil Affairs Functional Specialty Cells

The functional specialties are organized into functional specialty cells as shown in table 2. A Civil Affairs Command (CACOM), which serves as the theater level CA asset for the Geographic Combatant Command (GCC), provides three, 33 personnel functional specialty cells with all six of the functional specialty areas represented with the purpose of planning, coordinating, assessing or managing Civil Affairs Operations (CAO) depending on the mission. There are four CACOMs in the USAR inventory that are regionally aligned with the GCCs. One CACOM covers both the U.S. European Command (USEUCOM) and U.S. Africa Command (USAFRICOM) areas of operations. Two major functions of the CACOM are to provide a CA/Civil Military Operations planning and coordination capability to the GCC and the ability to form the core of a Joint Civil Military Operations Task Force (JCMOTF). The functional specialty cells are designed to be modular for general support of interagency operations or direct support of military operations. A deliberate decision was made to concentrate the functional specialist capability at the strategic level to provide the CA Commander the flexibility to support Joint Commanders in full-spectrum operations.[17] The USAR CA brigade and battalion organizations have one functional specialty cell with limited capabilities in four of the six functional areas. Economic stability and public education and information are not represented at the brigade and battalion levels in CA units.

To understand why the Civil Affairs functional specialty capability gap exists, we must review some of the history of how we got here. There are four main issues that have contributed to the CA functional specialty capability gap: high operational demand, changes in force structure and doctrine, proponent challenges, and restrictive personnel practices.

Operational Demand

Civil Affairs personnel and units have been in high demand for over two decades. In the 1990s, CA soldiers deployed to Kuwait, Haiti, Bosnia, and Kosovo. By the end of 2003, nearly half of the Army CA force strength (96% of which was in the Army Reserve at the time) was deployed in support of USCENTCOM missions.[18] By the beginning of 2004, it was evident that operations in Iraq and Afghanistan would last longer and require more reconstruction and stabilization efforts than originally envisioned. The demand for CA Soldiers in support of OIF and OEF plateaued at over 1100 personnel per rotation (every nine to ten months) or approximately 20% of its assigned strength.[19] This was a compromise that reduced the support for OEF and OIF by more than 50% of what was desired by conventional force commanders and required for support to Provincial Reconstruction Teams (PRTs), ad hoc organizations for civ-mil integration at the tactical level. Consequently, CA support was focused on tactical level support to maneuver commanders.[20]

While it was unknown how long OEF and OIF would last, it was clear that the projected demand for Civil Affairs would continue to outpace supply.[21] To meet the demand, internal cross leveling, the use of in lieu of individual augmentees from the Navy and Air Force, and rapidly retrained personnel from the Army Reserve to include the individual ready reserve were used heavily from 2005 to 2010. In 2007, the Secretary of Defense established planning objectives for utilization of the total force in order to provide predictability to service members, families, and for the RC, employers. The goal for the AC was established at one year deployed to two years at home (1:2) and involuntary mobilization for the RC at one year mobilized to every five years demobilized (1:5). As of 2008, the dwell ratios for Army Civil Affairs were active component at 1:08 and reserve component at 1:2.[22] It is important to note that the dwell ratio above can be misleading because it is for units not individuals. The spin rate for some individuals is likely higher. RC CA forces have not been fully manned and have used extensive cross leveling to fill battle rosters of unit flags that meet dwell requirements.

While growth has increased the number of units, particularly at the tactical level, there has not been an equivalent increase in the number of personnel at the mid-grade ranks. The potential negative impact of the sustained use of CA assets on recruiting and retention were identified as early as 2004.[23] The high operational demand caused many USAR Civil Affairs officers to leave the force in favor of focusing on their civilian professional careers and family.[24] Likewise, the high operational tempo was undoubtedly a barrier to recruiting the mid-grade civilian professionals needed to fill the functional specialty positions. As of September 2010, USAR Civil Affairs majors/captains were at 54% and 24% strength respectively.[25] Civil Affairs officer shortages mirror the officer shortage in the USAR writ large that has reached a critical level and threatens the long term health of the organization.[26] Because CA units cannot procure personnel directly from commissioning sources or civilian life, the pool of talented management level officers shrinks.[27] Officers in the reserves are increasingly likely to come from a narrow band of civilian backgrounds.[28] The experienced civil sector experts that are needed to fill functional specialist positions are in the category of persons that have the most conflict with the increased demands for reserve service.[29] Civilian skills that have traditionally been found in the RC vice the AC because of the availability of professional civilian acquired skills that can't be maintained in the AC may not exist in an operationally demanding RC force.

Force Structure and Doctrine

At the same time that CA was struggling to meet sourcing requirements for contingency operations, a force design update was approved that further deemphasized the functional specialties. The CA force converted from the "A-Series" to "G-Series" unit structure which "modularized" CA formations to better support the brigade combat team. Army transformation from a division centric force to a brigade centric force had wide ranging implications for the enabling forces. The conversion to a modular force pushed CA force structure to the tactical level by expanding the number of CA Companies while reducing the overall number of functional specialty positions.

The force structure change was accompanied by a corresponding change in doctrine that allocated each Brigade Combat Team (BCT), Theater Sustainment Brigade, and Maneuver Enhancement Brigade a Civil Affairs Company as a direct support unit when deployed. The CA force structure change was necessary in light of broader Army transformation and to better posture the force to meet high operational demand on a rotational basis. However, there were consequences for the CA functional specialist capability. In 1992, the functional specialties were approximately half of the CA force structure.[30] In 2001, the functional specialties were 36% of the total CA force structure. By 2015, when planned growth has been completed, the specialties will be 9% of the total CA force structure. The net loss of functional specialties positions as a result of the force design update and most recent growth is 998 positions or 18% of the 2001 authorized strength. The force design update deliberately concentrated functional specialists at the CA Brigade and CACOM levels to provide the CA Commander the flexibility to support Joint Commanders in full-spectrum operations.[31] Doctrinally, this construct provides an eight person team at the division level and no specialties at the BCT or provincial level where civilian support has increased to fill the gap.[32] Even if the functional specialists from a CA Battalion were pushed down to the BCT headquarters, this would only provide an eight person cell representing four of the six specialty areas.

For the 1st Calvary Division in Iraq, winning the peace involved "local infrastructure improvement, training security forces, understanding and educating the fundamentals of democracy, and creating long lasting jobs that would carry beyond short term infrastructure improvement."[33] In the absence of CA functional expertise, the division dedicated the engineer corps, enhanced by a robust pre-deployment training program with the Texas cities of Austin and Killeen, to deal with the complex tasks of maintaining a functioning city system as well as promotion of both the legitimacy and capacity of the Iraqi Government. Establishing basic local services and providing employment reduced the insurgent base of support and decreased attacks on U.S. Soldiers.

An analysis of the evolution of CA doctrine from the original manual, FM 27-5 *Basic Field Manual of Military Government*, published in July 1940 to present reveals major changes.[34] The 1940 manual deals primarily with the policy of military government and how military forces were to administer occupied territories. Subsequent CA manuals contained less content for how the military is to exercise its responsibilities to reestablish a viable government in accordance with international law. Post-Vietnam, Army doctrine returned to its preferred role of conventional warfare. The Army focused on the singular possibility of conventional combat in Germany against the Warsaw Pact forces. The civil military relationship was treated as a problem at the margins. Civil military operations concentrated primarily on population and resource control and support to host nation authorities. CA doctrine was focused on minimizing civilian interference with military operations. Most of the Civil Affairs units were configured to meet these requirements. CA doctrine still included aspects of low intensity conflict and civil administration; however, as priorities changed doctrine for full assumption of civil functions in enemy and friendly territory withered away.[35] Cold war thinking in the nuclear era suggested that there would be fewer total victories that would result in occupations.[36] As detailed doctrine on military governance disappeared so too did specific doctrine on the functional specialties. More recently, CA doctrine has not kept pace with current national security requirements for a strong CA functional specialty capability and capacity for stability and reconstruction.

Proponent Challenges

The Civil Affairs proponent has not been an adequate champion for updated doctrine, training and education, and personnel policies for the functional specialties. The current proponent for CA is the US Army John F. Kennedy Special Warfare Center and School (USAJFKSWCS).[37] The Commandant, USAJFKSWCS has proponent responsibilities for Special Forces and Military Information Support Operations (formerly Psychological Operations) in addition to CA. The proponent leaders assigned to execute the proponent functions are principally responsible for the Special Forces community who are naturally focused on their core special operations missions and execution of their congressionally directed activities. Consequently, the proponent's primary interest has been in Special Forces with low priority placed on force modernization considerations, vision, or advocacy for CA support to the general purpose force (GPF) or interagency support.[38] In the proponent's defense, CA representation at USAJFKSWCS has been woefully understaffed and without personnel with the requisite qualifications related to the functional specialties.[39] To make matters worse, CA proponent responsibilities have been distributed among various directorates of three different organizations: United States Special Operations Command (USASOC), United States Army Civil Affairs and Psychological Operations Command (USACAPOC), and USAJFKSWCS. USAJFKSWCS, until recently, was organized along functional lines rather than by branches further diluting CA branch advocacy within the larger proponent organization.

A proponent should develop doctrine that becomes a change agent, driving similar changes in organization, training, leader development, and the equipment and the type of forces built. Current CA manuals contain only a few paragraphs on support to civil administration in friendly and occupied territories and a few pages devoted to explaining the functional specialty areas but no doctrine on how to perform the functions. CA special texts that provided detailed guidance for the execution of each of the functional specialties in separate manuals were last published in the 1980s. In 1991, the Commandant, USAJFKSWCS reported that FM 41-11, a how to manual on the CA functions was in progress.[40] The manual, developed primarily by reserve personnel, was to have a chapter on each specialty area as well as separate annexes for recommended standards for qualifications and sustainment training.[41] For unknown reasons, this manual was never published.[42]

Current issues concerning CA functional specialists are not new. Concerns were raised by the Commandant, USAJFKSWCS as early as 1992. He asked questions that are still valid to this day, and have not been answered, some 20 years later.

"Are the current 20 functional specialties what CA and the military require for the future?

Do we have identifiable standards/qualifications for each of the functional specialties?

Are we able to track and identify what we have in the force?

How do we sustain these skills?

Do we have the capability that we say we have?"[43]

USACAPOC, the CA force provider, convened a working group to address these issues and made recommendations on the functional specialties, doctrine tasks, skill identifiers and standards, sustainment training, and force structure. As discussed previously, the doctrine was never published so sustainment training standards were not published or implemented. The only lasting legacy from the functional specialty review is the revision or development of skill identifiers for some of the functional specialty positions.[44] An issue that remains today is how best to define the standards for awarding the SIs to capture the skills required at each level (local, provincial, national) and how best to track the functional specialist skills resident in the force.[45] For example, a bank teller who may qualify for awarding of skill identifier 6C Economist by virtue of meeting the minimum experience requirement of five years in banking is probably not qualified to advise on how to set up a banking system at the national level.[46]

14

The functional specialty review working group felt that the skill identifiers were the best method for identifying and tracking the skills in the force. In order to be able to accurately track the skills, officers that meet the standards and qualification must submit for award of the appropriate SI. As of February 2010, there were only 38 officers assigned to Army Reserve CA units that had been awarded SIs for one of the 11 SIs that are currently in use on the USAR CA modified table of organization and equipment (MTOE).[47] Without polling the force, it is impossible to determine if all officers who meet the qualifications for one of the SIs have applied for and been awarded one. To fill the authorized CA functional specialty positions to 100% with true experts according to the current standards, the Army would need to recruit 271 officers covering all the specialty areas.

Personnel Policy

In 2005, the Defense Science Board, recognizing that DOD was "not sufficiently tapping into the capabilities and patriotism of our mid-career professional population", called for a change to the Army Reserve Civil Affairs recruitment process that would target more experienced professionals (35-45 years old) with the right skills needed for stability operations.[48] Current personnel policies and career management practices of the Army CA branch severely restrict the reserve force's ability to recruit and retain true experienced civil sector experts. As CA/MG gained recognition and development following WWII and Korea, the CA/MG USAR branch was established on August 17, 1955.[49] In 2006, the CA branch became an Army branch, recognizing the key role that both AC and RC CA officers play in not only fighting the war but winning the peace.[50] The new Army branch was heralded as a positive development to give active army officers greater career potential, more rewarding assignments, and greater recognition

15

for their unique expertise at a time when the active component force was growing to meet demand. The branch concept was designed to create interchangeability between AC and RC officers so that the origin of one was indistinguishable from another.[51] This is consistent with other Army branches and the total force concept. However, the application of a "one size fits all" approach to the accession and management of CA generalist and specialists negated the unique aspects of the former Army Reserve CA branch, namely, the incorporation of specialized civilian skills.[52] The RC CA generalists should be indistinguishable from their AC counterparts; however, there is no equivalent specialist capability in the AC CA force. Within all of the military services, force structure devoted to maintaining a ready pool of civil-sector functional expertise is a characteristic that is unique to Army Reserve Civil Affairs.[53] Army Reserve Civil Affairs' true value should be in its ability to access the necessary civilian acquired skills for stability operations, put those Soldiers in uniform and deploy them to do specific technical missions.[54]

The responsibility to recruit qualified individuals with civilian specialties currently falls on the USAR CA unit commander.[55] Too often unit commanders are "happy just to have bodies with the correct rank to fill slots, regardless of the civilian skills brought to the table."[56] The key to any human capital recruiting effort, civilian or military, is the application of appropriate resources to the effort proportional the results desired. The U.S. Army Recruiting Command recognized this when they stood up the Special Operations Recruiting Battalion (SORB) in 2005 to actively recruit candidates for service in Special Forces. In FY 2007, the mission was expanded to include active duty CA officers and enlisted. Unfortunately, since the USAR CA force had been realigned from

USASOC to the United States Army Reserve Command (USAR) in 2006, the SORB did not recruit for the RC CA force.

A consequence of the lack of true CA functional experts has forced the Civil Affairs community to substitute generalists or less than qualified individuals. The CA community recognizes that it has oversold its capability to deliver the required civilian skills; most CA soldiers are actually generalists.[57] The CA community should ask whether it is satisfied with CA operators who are primarily generalists and may have a minimal amount of basic knowledge and experience in the functional specialties of yesterday or does the 21st century operating environment required true civil sector experts to conduct stability operations across the full spectrum of conflict? The choice is clear. Stability operations are not a game for amateurs.[58] There is no substitute for skilled, experienced, and trained civil sector experts. The Army must address shortfalls in the CA forces' ability to catalyze a comprehensive approach to stability operations especially at the operational and strategic levels.

Way Ahead

There is no doubt that we must update doctrine, relook force structure, and develop training programs in order to address current functional specialist shortfalls. More important, though, is the effort to procure and develop human capital. The CA force must be able to obtain and develop highly qualified personnel to rebuild the functional specialty capability for the future.

A potential solution, therefore, as it relates to personnel policy warrants the creation of a distinct system for accessing and managing RC specialists. The creation of a separate branch or branches based on the Army Medical Department (AMEDD) model may best way to manage CA functional specialists. The RC CA specialists like

AMEDD officers require the development of single highly specialized skills rather than multiple skills identified in the dual track concepts of the Officer Personnel Management System (OPMS).[59] It may be difficult to create an effective career management model with appropriate development and promotion opportunities given the small number of specialists currently in the CA force structure. However, if implemented holistically, this recommendation could also address the issues identified with certifying, stratifying, and tracking the various specialty skills. It would also establish a framework against which the Army could apply recruiting resources to include incentives. The Army's current approach toward CA functional specialists is based on the flawed assumption that that Army Reserve CA units will be able to acquire enough highly qualified civil sector experts with the skills and experience required for one of the specialties in the absence of a systematic recruiting effort.

The CA proponent should first examine the position descriptions that the State Department's Civilian Response Corps (CRC) developed for its Active Response Corps in order to determine the specialty skills that are required.[60] Once those specialty skills have been determined, the proponent should ascertain the functional specialties required, determine from where to draw the civilian acquired skills, and develop qualification standards for the individual specialties. One excellent aid in this process could be data from a Rand Study which developed a methodology to identify the civilian skill sets required for stability tasks across each of the stability sectors, and then determined the occupations that possess the desired skill sets.[61]

The CRC has transformed to better integrate with the military in terms of sustainment, operations and planning, and force protection. Army CA should transform its functional specialist capability to better align with the existing civilian framework towards a whole of government staffing approach to planning and executing stability operations. A common civilian-military pool of civilian experts would increase interoperability for civ-mil teaming, allow for a common set of training standards, common techniques and procedures, and allow the USG to direct scarce civilian expertise to where it is needed most.[62] This approach would enable greater CA cooperation with the agencies it's most likely to work with in future operations.

As the Army shifted from an AirLand Battle doctrine focused on resisting the numerically superior Warsaw Pact armies to a post-cold war doctrine that treated combat and other operations separately to full spectrum operations doctrine that stresses the essentiality of integrating security, stability, and reconstruction with combat actions, Civil Affairs doctrine has not kept pace. Consideration should be given to better aligning the functional specialties and specialty areas with the five stability sectors and five essential stability tasks and articulating the role that functional specialists play in successful accomplishment in each of the five tasks across the full range of military operations as opposed to the traditional civil administration mission for which the specialties were originally conceived.

Civil Affairs functional specialty requirements should address the capability to advise, train, and assist at the local, provincial, and ministerial levels across the five stability sectors during phase 0 security cooperation missions. This is a scenario in which the functional specialists and CA in general have been underutilized primarily due to contingency operations demand and the GCC's inability to access the RC for more than a few training days at a time. As the Army implements the RC as an operational

19

force concept and draws down from large scale stability operations, building partner capacity is a mission for which the functional specialties are particularly well suited. However, to be most effective, the CA force and specialties may need to be adapted to the primary military role in this area. Doctrine analysts should examine the question of whether Civil Affairs functional specialties should have greater capability to support stability tasks in the security sector. The CA force could provide specialists (advisors, trainers, mentors, and liaison staff) in border control, law enforcement, legal and governance related to the ministries of defense, justice, and interior to help reform the HN security sector and build partner capacity to make it an enabler for long-term security.[63]

A 2008 HQDA DAMO-SSO internal study questioned if CA had "the capability and capacity to support the Army through all phases of Full Spectrum Operations in a Joint, Interagency and Multinational (JIM) environment."[64] The internal review recommended force structure changes to transform Army CA to support stability operations at the strategic and operational level. The concept called for transforming the existing functional specialty cells to create a CA Ministry Assistance Command (MAC) with regionally focused civ-mil teams designed to train, assist, and advise host nation ministries across the stability sectors. It is not clear where the civilians would come from for these teams. Nonetheless, the concept has merit. CA reservists with high level professional skills and advanced degrees formed ad hoc CA ministerial advisory teams to help restore or establish legitimate governments in Grenada, Panama, Kuwait, Haiti, Bosnia, Afghanistan, and Iraq.[65] At the strategic level, the MAT is a tool of the commander or ambassador to maintain stability, to assist in accomplishing foreign

policy objectives, and to fulfill the commander's legal responsibilities.[66]

Conclusion

The Civil Affairs functional specialist capability is an endangered species. The

Army can continue to go down the current path toward a generalized CA force or it can

decide to protect and preserve the specialized and uniquely valuable skills that citizen

soldiers can bring to the fight for stability. In an era of persistent conflict with a

constrained resource environment, the CA functional specialists in conjunction with the

CA force at large are the preferred means to implement an "innovative, low cost, small

foot print" approach that relies "on exercises, rotational presence, and advisory

capabilities" to meet our national security objectives. [67]

Endnotes

[1] U.S Department of Defense, *Military Support to Stabilization, Security, Transition, and Reconstruction Operations,* Joint Operating Concept Version 2.0 (Washington, DC: U.S. Department of Defense, December 2006), 13.

[2] U.S. Department of Defense, *Stability Operations*, Department of Defense Instruction 3000.05 (Washington, DC: U.S. Department of Defense, September 16, 2009), 2.

[3] The Department of Defense capabilities required follow from the Department of State (DOS) detailed stability focused, post conflict reconstruction task matrix that helps planners identify the specific requirements to support countries in transition from armed conflict or civil strife to sustained stability. The DOS stability sectors are security, justice and reconciliation, humanitarian and social well-being, governance and participation, and economic stabilization and infrastructure. The matrix offers visual proof of the complexity of stability operations, the multitude of tasks involved, and the difficulties inherent in forming an interagency approach to such operations. Office of Coordinator for Reconstruction and Stabilization, *Post-conflict Reconstruction Essential Tasks* (Washington, DC: Department of State, April 2005).

[4] U.S. Department of the Army, *Operations*, Field Manual 3-0 (Washington, DC: U.S. Department of the Army, 2008), viii.

[5] Army Stability Operations include five essential tasks: establish civil security, establish civil control, restore essential services, support to governance, and support to economic and infrastructure development. U.S. Department of the Army, *Unified Land Operations*, Army Doctrine Publication 3-0 (Washington, DC: U.S. Department of the Army, October 2011), 4.

[6] U.S. Army Training and Doctrine Command, *The United States Army Full Spectrum Operations Unified Quest 2007*, Training and Doctrine Command Pamphlet 525-5-300 (Fort Monroe, VA: U.S. Army Capabilities Integration Center, April 22, 2008), 37.

[7] The bulk of the Army's non-security related expertise in stability operations can be found in the Civil Affairs branch. An analysis of the 54 sectorial tasks in the DOS Essential Task Matrix (ETM) shows that Civil Affairs is the Army fallback capability for performing 75% of the tasks. Thomas S. Szayna et al., *Integrating Civilian Agencies in Stability Operations* (Washington, DC: The Rand Corporation, 2009), 11. A review of the subtasks associated with the five stability tasks in FM 3-07, reveals that CA has primary jurisdiction over four of the five tasks by virtue of the skills and experience demanded. Furthermore, these four tasks require skills that are not typically possessed by the combat arms branches that provide the bulk of the forces to the BCTs. The four primary stability tasks demand a high level of technical competence obtained through formal education and experience. Overall, the CA has branch primacy over 30 of the 38 subtasks. Kevin Burk, *Strategic Leadership in Stability Operations: A Challenge to Army Enterprise*, Strategic Research Project (Carlisle Barracks, PA: U.S. Army War College, March 30, 2010), 13.

[8] Office of the Undersecretary of Defense for Acquisition, Technology, and Logistics, *Report of the Defense Science Board on Institutionalizing Stability Operations Within DoD* (Washington, DC: Defense Science Board, September, 2005), 15.

[9] U.S. Department of Defense, *Report to Congress on the Implementation of DoD Directive 3000.05, Military Support to Stability, Security, Transition, and Reconstruction Operations* (Washington, DC: U.S. Department of Defense, April 1, 2007), 5.

[10] Chuck Donnell, "The Civil Affairs Force," briefing slides presented at 58th Annual Conference of the Association of Civil Affairs, Washington, DC, October 30, 2009.

[11] Simon Wosley, "Civil Affairs Future in the Stability Operations Environment, Army G-3/5-SSO Stability Operations," briefing slides, Washington, DC, November 3, 2007.

[12] U.S Department of Defense, *Report to Congress on Civil Affairs* (Washington, DC: Office of the Assistant Secretary of Defense for Special Operations, Low Intensity Conflict & Interdependent Capabilities, April 29, 2009), 6.

[13] The Department of Defense has recognized that civilian skills are a core competency of the reserve component at large. Citizen Soldiers, many of whom are corporate and community leaders bring their civilian acquired skills, talent, and experience with them. The blend of military and civilian skills possessed by reservists can be valuable not just to the Department of Defense but to other government agencies in their overseas missions, especially in stability activities. Commission on the National Guard and Reserves, *Transforming the National Guard and Reserves into a 21st-Century Operational Force*, Final Report to Congress and the Secretary of Defense (Arlington, VA: Commission on the National Guard and Reserves, January 31, 2008), 10. Soldiers involved in stabilization and reconstruction "must have a jack of all trades versatility and resourcefulness." Bruce B. Bingham, Daniel L. Rubini and Michael Cleary, "U.S. Army Civil Affairs-The Army's Ounce of Prevention," *The Land Warfare Papers*, No. 41 (March 2003): 3. The application of skills gained in the civilian sector in the performance of a military mission are usually serendipitous; however, and not the result of a systematic effort to apply a particular civilian skill for a specific military mission at a certain point in time. Despite identifying it as a

core competency, the Department of Defense has done little to track civilian skills to take full advantage of them for missions.

[14] U.S Department of Defense, *Report to Congress on Civil Affairs*, 12.

[15] CA core tasks are populace and resource control, foreign humanitarian assistance, civil information management, nation assistance, and support to civil administration. U.S. Department of the Army, *Civil Affairs Operations*, Field Manual 3-57 (Washington, DC: U.S. Department of the Army, October 31, 2011), 3-1.

[16] U.S. Department of the Army, Military Occupational Classification and Structure, Department of the Army Pamphlet 611-21 (Washington, DC: U.S. Department of the Army, January 22, 2007), Chapter 4.

[17] Kenneth R. Moore, "U.S. Army Reserve Civil Affairs Redesign FDU 05-01," briefing slides, Fort Bragg, NC, February 17, 2005; U.S. Department of the Army, *Civil Affairs Operations*, Field Manual 3-57 (Washington, DC: U.S. Department of the Army, October 31, 2011), 1-8.

[18] Hugh C. Van Roosen, *Implications of the 2006 Reassignment of U.S. Army Civil Affairs*, Strategy Research Project (Carlisle Barracks, PA: U.S. Army War College, March 30, 2009), 3.

[19] Hugh C. Van Roosen, *Implications of the 2006 Reassignment of U.S. Army Civil Affairs*, 4.

[20] David N. Blackledge, "Commanders Emergency Response Program", briefing transcript, Coalition Provisional Authority, Iraq, January 14, 2004, http://www.defense.gov/transcripts/transcript.aspx?transcriptid=1417 (accessed January 23, 2012).

[21] Kathleen H. Hicks and Christine E. Wormuth, *The Future of U.S. Civil Affairs* (Washington, DC: Center for Strategic and International Studies, February 2009), 40.

[22] U.S Department of Defense, *Report to Congress on Civil Affairs*, 18.

[23] R. Christian Brewer, *U.S. Army Civil Affairs and the Fate of Reserve Special Operations Forces in Support of Current and Future Operations*, Strategy Research Project (Carlisle Barracks, PA: U.S. Army War College, March 19, 2004), 5.

[24] William R. Florig, "Theater Civil Affairs Soldiers A Force at Risk," *Joint Forces Quarterly*, no. 43 (4th Quarter 2006): 61.

[25] U.S. Army John F. Kennedy Special Warfare Center and School Directorate of Special Operations Proponency, "Civil Affairs Growth," briefing slides, Fort Bragg, NC, December 9, 2010.

[26] Ernest Erlandson, *An Institution in Crisis: The Army Reserve Officer Corps*, Strategy Research Project (Carlisle Barracks, PA: U.S. Army War College, February 16, 2009), 13.

[27] George B. McDonnell, *Civil Affairs – Vanguard for the Emerging Army Reserve Profession*, Strategy Research Project (Carlisle Barracks, PA: U.S. Army War College, January 3, 2009), 18.

[28] Charles C. Moskos, *The Sociology of The Army Reserves: Final Report* Army Research Institute Research Note 90-88 (Alexandria, VA: U.S. Army Research Institute for Behavior and Social Sciences, July 1990), 7.

[29] Dallas D. Owens, "From Reserve to Full Partner: Transforming the Reserve Professionals" in *The Future of the Army Profession*, 2nd edition, ed. Don M. Snider and Lloyd J. Mathews (New York, McGraw Hill, 2005), 567.

[30] Douglas K. Meyer, *Civil Affairs Functional Specialty Review* (Fort Bragg, NC: U.S. Army John F. Kennedy Warfare Center and School, December 9, 1993), 3.

[31] Kenneth R. Moore, "U.S. Army Reserve Civil Affairs Redesign FDU 05-01," briefing slides, Fort Bragg, NC, February 17, 2005.

[32] Richard Unda, *Rethinking the Use of Specialized Civil Affairs*, Strategy Research Project (Carlisle Barracks, PA: U.S. Army War College, November 5, 2009), 9.

[33] Peter W. Chiarelli and Patrick R. Michaels, "The Requirement for Full-Spectrum Operations," *Military Review* (July-August, 2005): 4.

[34] Hugh Van Roosen, *Should Military Government Return to its Roots?*, Student Issue Paper (Carlisle Barracks, PA: Center for Strategic Leadership, U.S. Army War College, August 2009), 1.

[35] Thijs W. Brocades Zaalberg, *Soldiers and Civil Power* (Amsterdam: Amsterdam University Press, 2006), 68.

[36] Wally Z. Walters, *The Doctrinal Challenge of Winning the Peace Against Rogue States: How Lessons from Post-World War II Germany May Inform Operations Against Saddam Hussein's Iraq*, Strategy Research Project (Carlisle Barracks, PA: U.S. Army War College, April 9, 2002), 26.

[37] The United States Army John F. Kennedy Special Warfare Center and School (USAJFKSWCS) has been the Civil Affairs proponent since the early 1970's when the U.S. Army Civil Affairs School, which had been at Fort Gordon, GA since 1955 was moved to Fort Bragg and consolidated with the U.S. Army Institute for Military Assistance (USAIMA). The USAIMA later became the U.S. Army John F. Kennedy Special Warfare Center and School. On June 20, 1990, USAJFKSWCS was reassigned from TRADOC to the U.S. Army Special Operations Command. The department of the Army assigns force modernization proponents to be the change agents for particular functions or branches in order to transform the Army. Force modernization proponents are responsible for determining and integrating doctrine, organization, training, materiel, leadership and education, personnel, and facilities (DOTMLPF) requirements. A branch proponent is the commandant or the chief of a branch of the Army with responsibility for execution of training, leader development, education, and providing recommendations on the personnel life cycle appropriate to their branch. Civil Affairs, an Army Reserve branch since 1959, and an Army branch since 2006, is one of only three branches that

does not have a branch chief to serve as an advocate on its behalf (the other two being special forces and psychological operations). U.S. Department of the Army, *The Army Force Modernization Proponent System*, Army Regulation 5-22 (Washington, DC: Headquarters Department of the Army, February 6, 2009).

[38] The Civil Affairs Association, *Civil Affairs Issue Papers*, (Columbia, MD: The Civil Affairs Association, November 2007), 3-1.

[39] CA proponent shortcomings received the attention of the Army only after it was directed to stand up a new AC CA Brigade to become part of the general purpose force (GPF). The Army Staff examined the appropriateness of CA proponent placement as well as its resource requirements to properly support the total force. Army G3/5/7 concerns about the Civil Affairs (CA) proponent issues which could negatively impact projected CA growth led to Army Campaign Plan (ACP) Decision Point (DP) 136 in June of 2009 to look at where the force modernization responsibilities for the CA force should reside. Rather than attempting to move or shift the proponent and potentially impact the force generation schedule through 2014, it was decided instead to provide the USAJFKSWCS with the resources necessary to successfully execute the required force generation and proponent functions. DP 136 was closed and the Army staff opened DP 153 titled Enabling Civil Affairs in January 2010. DP 153 resulted in a decision to implement a resourcing strategy for CA that included an increase in personnel for proponent support and unfunded requirements budget estimates to resource the proponent through FY 13. A request for a General Officer billet to serve as the Army CA Branch proponent was not approved. The deficiencies in the Army Reserve functional specialties were not a subject of either DP. There are still concerns at Department of the Army Secretariat level that the current proponent situation has separated the active and reserve component CA force and is therefore no longer tenable. U.S Department of the Army Assistant Secretary Manpower and Reserve Affairs Thomas R. Lamont, "Subject: Military Government and Civil Affairs Force Management and Branch Proponent, Washington, DC, June 1, 2011.

[40] David J. Baratto, "From the Commandant," *Special Warfare* 4, no. 1 (Winter 1991).

[41] Douglas K. Meyer, *Civil Affairs Functional Specialty Review*, 11.

[42] Brad Striegel, *Civil Affairs Functional Specialty Review* (Fort Bragg, NC: December 17, 2009) 17.

[43] Douglas K. Meyer, *Civil Affairs Functional Specialty Review*, 1.

[44] Brad Striegel, *Civil Affairs Functional Specialty Review,* 9.

[45] Vice Chairman of the Joint Chiefs of Staff Admiral James A. Winnefeld, Jr. "Subject: Civil Affairs (CA) DOTMLPF Change Recommendation," Washington, DC, December 1, 2011.

[46] Mark L. Kimmey, "Transforming Civil Affairs," *Army*, March 2005: 17-25; William R. Florig, "Theater Civil Affairs Soldiers A Force at Risk," *Joint Forces Quarterly*, no. 43 (4th Quarter 2006): 60-63.

[47] Jeremy Burque, "Civil Affairs Skill Identifiers," briefing Slides, Fort Bragg, NC, U.S. Army John F. Kennedy Special Warfare Center and School DSOP, February 2010.

[48] Office of the Undersecretary of Defense for Acquisition, Technology, and Logistics, *Report of the Defense Science Board on Institutionalizing Stability Operations Within DoD* (Washington, DC: Defense Science Board, September, 2005), 48.

[49] In 1959, the Army redesigned the branch Civil Affairs dropping the military government. The branch retained the skills and experience of CA officers that previously were required to serve with their basic branches if mobilized. Stanley Sandler, *Glad to See Them Come and Sorry to See Them Go: A History of U.S. Army Tactical Civil Affairs/Military Government, 1775-1991* (Fort Bragg, NC: U.S. Army Special Operations Command History and Archives Division, n.d.), 337.

[50] Previously, the AC equivalent to the USAR CA branch had been Functional Area 39. Curtis Boyd, "CA and PSYOP: Major Changes in Personnel, Training Upcoming for Officers, NCOs," *Special Warfare* (July 2005): 20.

[51] Boyd, "CA and PSYOP: Major Changes in Personnel, Training Upcoming for Officers, NCOs," 21.

[52] Office of the Undersecretary of Defense for Acquisition, Technology, and Logistics, *Report of the Defense Science Board on Institutionalizing Stability Operations Within DoD* (Washington, DC: Defense Science Board, September, 2005), 48.

[53] The Civil Affairs Association, *Civil Affairs Issue Papers*, (Columbia, MD: The Civil Affairs Association, November 2007), 2-2.

[54] Bingham, Rubini and Cleary, "U.S. Army Civil Affairs-The Army's Ounce of Prevention," 8.

[55] In the Army reserve, time is perhaps the most precious resource of all. Recruitment of Soldiers with specific civilian acquired skills competes with the myriad of other important command responsibilities. Unlike all other accession programs, there are no institutional resources devoted to the effort of recruiting Army Reserve CA Officers. Furthermore, Civil Affairs is a non-accessions branch with no direct commission authority to bring in specialists directly from civilian life. The candidates must already be a member of the Army Reserve in another Army branch and be willing to transfer to Civil Affairs. Personnel policies further restrict the pool of candidates by requiring that they be in the grade of First Lieutenant or Captain. In the RC, recruiting is also limited by geography. Members of the RC are limited by policy to membership in units within 50 miles of their home of record unless they are willing to travel greater distances at their own expense. Functional specialty positions in the USAR are concentrated at eight brigades, two of which are located outside of the continental U.S (Hawaii and Germany), and four CA Commands further limiting the number possible locations where members could serve in positions related to their civilian specialty.

[56] Florig, "Theater Civil Affairs Soldiers A Force at Risk," 61.

[57] Mark L. Kimmey, "Transforming Civil Affairs," *Army*, March 2005: 17-25; William R. Florig, "Theater Civil Affairs Soldiers A Force at Risk," *Joint Forces Quarterly*, no. 43 (4th Quarter 2006): 60-63; Richard Unda, *Rethinking the Use of Specialized Civil Affairs*, Strategy Research Project (Carlisle Barracks, PA: U.S. Army War College, November 5, 2009).

[58] Robert M. Perito, "Provincial Reconstruction Teams in Iraq," *United States Institute of Peace Special Report*, no. 185 (March 2007): 10.

[59] U.S. Department of the Army, *Army Medical Department Officer Development and Career Management*, Department of the Army Pamphlet 600-4 (Washington, DC: Department of the Army, June 27, 2007), 1.

[60] Todd Goehler, "G-35-SSO Internal Study Army Civil Affairs in Full Spectrum Operations," briefing slides with scripted commentary, Washington, DC, HQDA DAMO-SSO, February 21, 2008.

[61] Thomas S. Szayna et al., *Integrating Civilian Agencies in Stability Operations* (Arlington, VA: RAND Corporation, 2009), 66.

[62] Ibid.,154.

[63] U.S. Joint Chiefs of Staff, *Stability Operations*, Joint Publication 3-07 (Washington, DC: U.S. Joint Chiefs of Staff, September 29, 2011), C-1.

[64] Todd Goehler, "G-35-SSO Internal Study Army Civil Affairs in Full Spectrum Operations," briefing slides with scripted commentary, Washington, DC, HQDA DAMO-SSO, February 21, 2008.

[65] U.S Department of Defense, *Report to Congress on Civil Affairs*, 12.

[66] Bingham, Rubini and Cleary, "U.S. Army Civil Affairs-The Army's Ounce of Prevention," 9.

[67] Barrack Obama, *Sustaining US Global Leadership: Priorities for 21st Century Defense* (Washington, DC: U.S. Department of Defense, January 2012), 3.